SUPER STORMS
that rocked the world
HURRICANES, TSUNAMIS, AND OTHER DISASTERS

Written by **Mark Shulman**   Designed by **On-Purpos, Inc.**

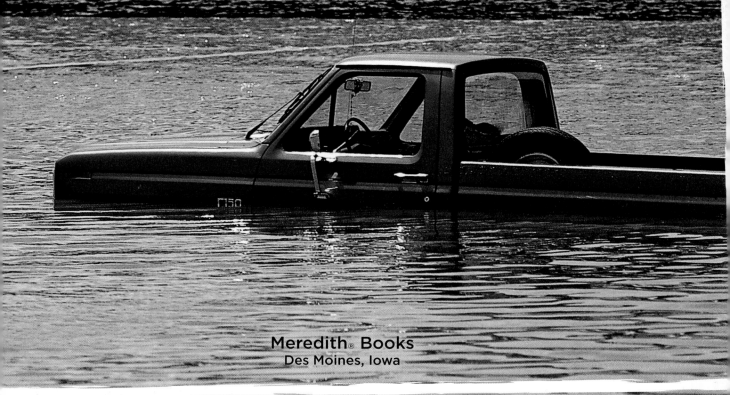

Meredith® Books
Des Moines, Iowa

Jane Root, President & General Manager, Discovery Channel
Carol LeBlanc, Vice President, Licensing
Elizabeth Bakacs, Vice President, Creative Services
Brigid Ferraro, Director, Licensing
Caitlin Erb, Licensing Specialist

www.discovery.com

Meredith Books
1716 Locust St.
Des Moines, IA 50309-3023
meredithbooks.com

First Edition.

Manufactured and printed in the United States of America.
ISBN 978-0-696-23702-7

Photo credits:
© Don Farrall/Getty Images, cover; FEMA/NOAA News Photo, cover (inset), page 22 (inset); Mark Wolfe/FEMA, page 37 (top inset); © Warren Faldley/CORBIS, pages 1-3; Jocelyn Augustino/ FEMA, pages 4, 37, back cover (inset, left); Jim Bowers/U.S. Geological Survey, pages 4 (inset), 38 (inset); NASA/DART, page 26 (inset); Andrea Booher/FEMA, pages 5, 28-29, 32-33; National Oceanic and Atmospheric Administration (NOAA) pages 5 (inset); 6-7, 12-13, 14-15, 16-17, 20-21, back cover (inset, right); Department of Defense Photo, page 8; U.S. Geological Survey Photographic Library, pages 9, 18, 19 (inset); J.D. Wheeler Photo, Robert E. Lee Collection, pages 10-11; Hebei Provincial Seismological Bureau, U.S. Geological Survey, page 19; © Alex L. Fradkin/age fotostock, page 22; © Robert Madden/ National Geographic Image Collection, page 23; N. Banks/U.S. Geological Survey, page 24-25 (top); T. Pierson/U.S. Geological Survey, page 25 (bottom); © Leverette Bradley/CORBIS, page 26; United States Department of Agriculture, page 27; © CP/Robert Galbraith, page 30; © AP/Wide World Photos, page 31 (inset); © Steven Collins/Shutterstock.com, page 34; David Rydevik, page 35; Liz Roll/FEMA, page 36; Pam Irvine/ California Geological Survey, page 38

CONTENTS

WHAT A

DISASTER!

First people build something. Then nature destroys it. This pattern hasn't changed since humans lived in caves and worried about landslides. Or earthquakes. Or hurricanes. Or floods. Or sometimes all of the above, all at the same time.

Welcome to Earth. It's a beautiful place, but it sure knows how to rock our world now and then.

Inside *Super Storms That Rocked the World*, you'll find information about all sorts of memorable natural disasters from the past century and the last few years. Each earth-shattering true story describes in detail the great destruction, devastation, and debris. But you'll also find details of the daringness, drive, and determination it takes of people to dig out and start over. That's the way it's always been, and that's the way it will always be.

Now grab your thermometer (for the cold), your anemometer (for the wind), your seismometer (for the earthquakes), your rain gauge (sorry, it's not an –ometer), and your copy of *Super Storms That Rocked the World* . . . and let's go!

Hang on to your planet. It's a wild ride!

1896
GREAT CYCLONE
AT ST. LOUIS

It lasted only 15 minutes from start to finish. But it shook St. Louis, Missouri, and East St. Louis, Illinois, forever. At 4:30 p.m. on May 27, 1896, temperatures suddenly dropped as enormous black clouds confronted the city. Winds picked up quickly and dangerously. The lightning came, then the thunder, followed by torrential sheets of rain. Anyone caught on the streets, on a streetcar, or inside an unsafe building in the tornado's path would soon be caught in the hands of fate.

Nearly 9,000 buildings were wrecked, ruined, or ripped apart. Well-built houses were lifted or leveled. Railroad cars were destroyed or derailed. Several steamboats sank. Trolley cars were carried off. Large, solid trees were torn apart and thrown. Bridges were broken. Hundreds of miles of gas and electric lines were severed. Thousands of telephone and telegraph poles were destroyed. It was the first major disaster of the electric age and the first great tornado whose damage would be photographed.

OFF THE CHARTS

Even by tornado standards, this one was massive: Its path of destruction was more than a mile wide. Modern estimates put the winds at F4 ("devastating damage," up to 260 miles per hour) or even F5 ("incredible damage," up to 318 mph) on the Fujita scale.

ONE OF MANY

This enormous twister was just one of several tornadoes to strike Missouri and Illinois that May day. In today's dollars, the damage to the large, wealthy St. Louis area was more than $3 billion. It was the third deadliest tornado in U.S. history.

1906

SAN FRANCISCO EARTHQ

HEADING SOUTH

San Francisco wasted no time getting back to business. New buildings, better roads, and even a subway arrived in the quake's aftermath. By 1915, the city hosted the lavish Panama-Pacific International Exposition, with the destruction forgotten. When the next major earthquake hit San Francisco in 1989, the city was prepared.

UP FROM THE ASHES

The 1906 earthquake was felt almost 400 miles south, in Los Angeles. After 1906, nervous folks made Los Angeles the most populous city on the West Coast. Of course, Los Angeles has had a few quakes of its own.

QUAKE

April 18, 1906, was a day like any other—at least for the first five hours. But at 5:12 a.m., San Francisco was shaken by the earthquake that caused the worst destruction ever recorded in North America.

Roofs collapsed. Walls disintegrated. Solid stone buildings crumbled to the ground. Roads cracked open and swallowed trees, houses, and whatever else was up above. More than 500 city blocks were destroyed. And no wonder: The epicenter of this tremendous quake (estimated at a devastating 7.8 on the Richter scale) was just 2 miles from the most populous city on the West Coast.

Still, the shifting of Earth's tectonic plates wasn't what caused the most destruction. Up to 90 percent of the damage was caused by the fires that raged throughout the city. Ruptured natural gas mains (gas was a major source of heat and lighting) caused many blazes. Arson was also a significant factor. The army was called in to restore order and to help stop the fire by using dynamite to detonate—and remove—blocks of buildings from the fire's path before they could burn. Of the more than 400,000 residents of San Francisco at that time, nearly 300,000 lost their homes.

LEFT BEHIND

Not surprisingly, the survivors of the Wellington Avalanche wanted to put the tragedy behind them. Less than a year later, they renamed the town Tye, for the river below it. But that solution was short-lived. In 1929, after the second Cascade Railroad Tunnel was opened, the town had no more purpose and was abandoned. It's now one of the ghost towns of Washington.

AVALAN

WELLINGTON, WA

1910

On February 23, 1910, two eastbound trains on the Great Northern Railway were carrying more than 100 people through the state of Washington. Heavy snow forced them to stop outside the small town of Wellington, beneath the peak of Windy Mountain. After six days of blizzards and heavy snow, a rainstorm filled the mountain air with thunder.

That's how the nation's deadliest avalanche began. At 1 a.m. on March 1, a violent thunderclap broke loose a massive wall of snow a quarter-mile wide and a half-mile deep. The powerful avalanche charged forward, rumbling toward the town and the trains. There were no trees to stop the deluge of snow: A recent forest fire had left the slopes bare and vulnerable. The avalanche missed the town's hotel/general store/post office by only a few hundred feet. But the trains and the depot were thrown downhill, crushed, and buried under 10 feet of unforgiving snow. The force of the avalanche twisted the metal trains and shoved their wrecked hulls more than 150 feet into the river valley below.

Railroad employees in the hotel rushed to rescue as many survivors as they could. Unfortunately the hazardous weather conditions slowed rescue efforts, which weren't complete until late spring, when the thaw made it possible to reclaim the victims and salvage the remains of the trains.

MISSISSIPPI RIVER
FLOOD

1927

EXODUS

More than 700,000 people became refugees crowded into 150 camps. And thousands of African-Americans pulled up stakes to begin another great northern migration.

I t makes sense that America's greatest river flood took place on America's greatest river. When the Mississippi River flooded on April 16, 1927, protective levees failed all along the system in six states: Illinois, Kentucky, Tennessee, Arkansas, Mississippi, and Louisiana. How could this have happened?

The Central Mississippi Basin had been deluged with constant rainstorms during the summer of 1926, leaving the river vulnerable to flooding. On New Year's Day in 1927, further rains caused water to slop over the edges of levees. More swells in March and April followed heavy rains, and on April 16, an 8-inch downpour pushed the strained flood walls to the brink. Just south of Cairo, Illinois, a quarter-mile section of levee collapsed, plunging 275 square miles of land under 10 feet of water. And that was just the beginning.

The surging waters headed south with the Mississippi's current, and towns on both sides of the river nervously prepared for the worst. Arkansas was badly damaged, with nearly 15 percent of its land submerged. Witnesses compared the water surging through the break in the levee near Greenville, Mississippi, to the force of Niagara Falls. In different locations, lakes of water formed up to 90 miles inland. Before the torrent could flood majestic New Orleans, the city dynamited the levee at Caernarvon farther south, flooding poorer communities instead.

GREAT COVERAGE

From Tennessee southward, the river swelled to more than 60 miles wide. Eventually the river overran its levees in 145 places from north to south, covering 26,000 square miles of formerly dry land.

1930s

DUST B

CAUGHT IN THE WRATH

As many as 500,000 forlorn people permanently migrated west to California from Oklahoma and neighboring states. They loaded up old trucks and horse-drawn wagons, and some even walked more than 1,500 miles.

What caused the tremendous devastation of America's Dust Bowl in the 1930s? Bad planning and bad luck. The bad planning was the fault of poor farmers. They destroyed vast amounts of grassland in the midwestern and southern Plains states by continuing to grow crops in overused, weak soil. The bad luck was several years of long and severe droughts. It dried the exposed soil to dust. In 1931 when the notorious Plains winds whipped up as usual, enormous dark clouds of dust choked the skies.

And the rains kept refusing to fall. More crops died, more farms failed, more dust rose, and sky-blackening clouds became a deadly fact of life. By 1934 the drought was officially the worst in U.S. history. Twenty-seven states were severely affected, and 75 percent of the country was covered in dust. More than 35 million acres of farmland were destroyed. There was terrible poverty from coast to coast because this all happened during the worst of the Great Depression. Yet millions of cattle and other livestock had to be slaughtered, as they were unfit to eat due to starvation.

1935 saw the worst of these "black blizzards," and Congress declared the situation a "national menace." Several farming laws were passed. President Roosevelt developed programs to bail out desperate farm families, but by that point, the land was too weak to grow any plants. A billion tons of vital topsoil had blown across the country and out to sea. The drought and desperation continued until 1939, when the rains finally reappeared, nourishing the land and bringing wheat and other crops back to the American Plains.

1969

HURRICA

CAMILLE

NE

The United States has seen its share of hurricanes, tornadoes, cyclones, and serious windstorms. But no storm in American history has ever been as destructive as Hurricane Camille. The storm first slammed Cuba as a Category 3 hurricane on August 14, 1969, then picked up speed and raged on a northwesterly path toward the U.S. By the time this tropical cyclone reached the Gulf Coast states, it had accelerated to the lethal Category 5 status. So rare are hurricanes of this magnitude, only three attacked the U.S. during the entire 20th century. And of these, Camille was the worst.

On August 17, when Camille made landfall in coastal Louisiana, winds were clocked beyond 200 mph—powerful enough to lift trees and flatten wooden buildings. Hurricane-force winds of at least 160 mph lasted 10 hours or more. Cars flipped over and power lines were crippled. The lethal winds thrashed; heavy rains caused flooding along the coast. Boats, docks, and offshore oil rigs were also demolished by the surging storm tides that raised water levels about 25 feet. The hardest hit region, Harrison County, Mississippi, reported 68 square miles of total destruction. In today's dollars, the destruction cost more than $8 billion. Sadly, most of the victims could have been saved, but they refused the order to evacuate.

FLASH NORTH

By the time Camille left the South and headed up to Virginia on August 19, the winds had died down to 120 mph but rains increased—thrashing Virginia's Nelson County area with more than 30 inches of rain in less than five hours. The resulting flash floods caused nearly as much damage as the heavier winds down south. Nearly 14,000 homes were damaged and more than 5,600 were destroyed.

TANGSHAN EARTHQUAKE 1976

The most catastrophic earthquakes do the worst damage if they strike a city. In modern history, many had come close, but none dead-on . . . until the great earthquake struck Tangshan in China. At about 3:45 a.m. on July 28, 1976, this city of 1 million was overcome by a devastating quake whose impact was between 7.8 and 8.2 on the Richter scale.

The sleeping city had no chance to duck for cover. When the deadly 15 seconds of tremors were over, tens of thousands of buildings were lost, from houses and stores to hospitals and government buildings. Most roads were destroyed. The next afternoon brought more disaster: An aftershock of 7.1, nearly as lethal as the first quake, ripped the city again. Many perished who were still trapped in their crushed homes. All in all, 20 square miles of city were reduced to rubble. Several more aftershocks followed, each a significant earthquake in itself.

There weren't warning tremors before the quake, but Tangshan survivors observed clues from nature. On the day before the earthquake, sudden bursts of sound and light (including fireballs) were witnessed at night. Meanwhile, wells began cracking, gas was seen shooting out of wells, and water levels rose and fell a number of times. The animals also felt the impending doom. Chickens refused to eat. Geese began running and honking wildly. Mice and weasels ran for cover, all before a single tremor was felt.

AKE

DISASTER TOLL

Water, electricity, gas, telephone service, and transportation were severely disrupted. And when the tremors finally ceased, more than 250,000 people had died, and 165,000 more were severely injured. It was the deadliest earthquake of the 20th century.

1977
BUFFALO, NY
BLIZZA

Between January 28 and February 1, 1977, the city of Buffalo, New York, and nearby areas were struck by a very powerful, very dangerous blizzard. Just after 11 a.m. on Friday, January 28, temperatures quickly dropped 26 degrees (to 0°F) as a blinding wall of snow approached the city. Winds gusted to about 70 mph, and visibility was often zero. Emergency clearance vehicle drivers couldn't see their own plows. Within two hours, 18 inches of snow had fallen. The first night, drifts up to 15 feet high swallowed the roads. The city shut down.

It wasn't all new snow. A month of colder-than-average temperatures had left more than 5 feet of powdery snow along frozen Lake Erie—snow the blizzard winds carried right to Buffalo. The deadly combination of deep snow, brutal winds, and extreme cold left more than 10,000 vehicles (and their owners) stranded. Driving was banned. Snowmobiles were loaned to emergency crews and to more than 500 National Guardsmen, who had been dispatched. Fire trucks froze at fire scenes for weeks as the temperature reached a record low –7°F. The wind chill made it feel even colder: –40°F.

It took awhile for the blizzard's effects to melt away. By February 9, after 45 straight days of freezing temperatures, the mercury finally reached 34°F. By February 11, the driving ban was eased, and by February 14, students returned to school after missing 10 days.

BURIED ALIVE

On January 30, hundreds of drivers came out in the short-lived sun, only to get stranded by major snow squalls later that day. Then even snowmobiles were banned. President Jimmy Carter declared the nation's first-ever snow-related federal disaster. Construction vehicles, which were better at plowing snow, were called out in force. So were more than 300 army troops. In nearby rural areas, drifts more than 20 feet high caused people to leave their homes from upstairs windows.

MOUNT ST. HELENS
ERUPT

1980

here had been plenty of warning. For two months, hundreds of earthquakes had rumbled through Washington state from the base of Mount St. Helens volcano. Steam vents in the ground exploded several times, sending scalding blasts of ash nearly 2 miles into the atmosphere. Magma bubbled close to the surface, and blue gas flames burst upward. Craters opened. And as the locals began their evacuation, the nation watched.

But no amount of warning could prepare them for what came next. On May 18, 1980, at 8:32 a.m., an earthquake measuring 5.1 on the Richter scale shook the region. The whole north face of the volcano broke free, creating an avalanche of solid rock covering 17 miles. Molten lava and rocks escaped from the broken surface and exploded high into the air. More than 500 million tons of ash covered the area and eventually traveled to 10 other states. The heat melted glaciers, snow, and ice, causing severe mud slides that covered several hundred square miles, destroying much that the lava and earthquakes had spared. The energy of the explosion was the equivalent of 25,000 atomic bombs.

It was the greatest and deadliest volcanic eruption ever recorded in the continental United States. Eruptions and earthquakes continued the next day and occasionally throughout the year. Great areas of land were demolished, thousands of animals perished, and more than $1 billion worth of property was ruined, including hundreds of homes, dozens of bridges, railways, and highways. And the mountain, now 1,300 feet shorter, was scarred with a 2-mile gash of a crater forever . . . or at least until its next eruption.

1985

Nevado del Ruiz, in the Andes mountains of South America, is just 50 miles west of Bogotá, the capital city of Colombia. It is a stratovolcano, meaning its steep (17,784 ft.) cone is made of lava and ash that piled up after more than 6,000 years of eruptions. Even with its dangerous reputation, more than 28,000 Columbians lived in Armero, a nearby town. That is, until the volcano changed the area forever.

On November 13, 1985, Colombia experienced its deadliest volcanic disaster in 430 years. But it began almost peacefully. The warm orange glow on the mountaintop had become a familiar sight to local residents. A few days before the eruption, white clouds of steam appeared over the peak of the volcanic mountain. People had become accustomed to slight tremors as well. The familiar signs of volcanic activity hadn't mobilized the population because certain "experts" assured people there was no danger.

The early-morning explosion rocked the region. Millions of tons of lava mixed with melted snow and ice, creating lahars—massive, hot mudflows of deadly sludge—more than 150 feet thick. Imagine an endlessly wide 15-story building coming at you. These lahars followed valleys in several directions for 60 miles or more, burying everything. The town of Armero, 45 miles away, had been built on the ash of the previous eruption in 1845. Now more than 5,000 homes and nearly everything else were lost. According to sources, the volcanic avalanche was indiscriminate, demolishing one building and sparing its next-door neighbor.

NEVADO DEL RUIZ
VOLCANIC

CHAIN REACTION

To add to the horror, the heat of the lahars attracted microscopic life forms that caused often fatal infections in thousands more people. When it was finally over, three-fourths of the population of Armero had perished. The survivors were mostly injured and permanently relocated. But newer, better, more scientific means of detecting the next eruption were finally put into place.

ERUPTION

1991

FIRE

ASHES TO ASHES

Entire neighborhoods were decimated, with nearly 3,000 houses and apartments destroyed at a cost of more than $1.5 billion. The neighborhoods are completely rebuilt now, following new building regulations, but every autumn, the Diablo winds blow again.

STORM

OAKLAND, CA

They're called the Diablo winds—the Devil winds—and they blow dry, hot, and lethal every autumn in northern California. The Oakland hills around San Francisco are a potential fire hazard at the best of times, but while the Diablo winds are blowing, they're downright dangerous.

By 1991, the Oakland area had experienced a five-year drought. On October 19, 1991, firefighters extinguished a 5-acre grass fire in Wildcat Canyon. The next day, the fire reignited and rode the 50 mph Diablo winds across the Oakland hills, claiming an entire apartment building as its first victim. It moved outward from there, jumping highways and scorching homes in every direction. At first the fire followed the winds to the northeast. But as with any true firestorm, it began to create its own wind too. The fire's winds and the Diablo winds combined forces, generating lethal, powerful gusts that pushed flames and sparks farther into the abundant dry scrub and wood in the area.

These "perfect storm" conditions made firefighting efforts impossible for nearly 12 hours, until the wind stopped. Firefighters from local brigades, the U.S. Department of Forestry, the Naval Air Station, and even NASA coordinated the response. It took three full days to bring the fires under control and nine days to defeat them.

When the flames finally were extinguished on October 28, the Oakland firestorm had become one of the largest and costliest fires in U.S. history. More than 1,500 acres of land—covering 2.5 square miles—were thoroughly charred.

1993

GREAT
MIDWEST F

OOD

I t was one of the most destructive natural disasters ever to strike the United States. It overwhelmed nine states with record flooding. It caused up to $20 billion in damage. And it occurred less than 15 years ago. What happened?

The Great Midwest Flood of 1993 began during the winter of 1992, which had been especially snowy. The following spring and summer saw constant heavy rains as well. In Des Moines, Iowa, a record 48 inches of rain fell between April 1 and August 31, overwhelming the Des Moines and Raccoon rivers. With places receiving 350 percent more rainfall than usual, the flood defense systems of the Mississippi and the Missouri rivers were constantly near flood stage. These rivers, and about 150 lesser waterways, simply became overwhelmed.

In June, Wisconsin was flooded. On July 12, the Mississippi crested in St. Louis, Missouri. The states of Illinois, Iowa, Kansas, Minnesota, Missouri, Nebraska, North Dakota, South Dakota, and Wisconsin were in states of emergency. Levees failed. Bridges were washed out. Hundreds of communities were evacuated, and more than 75 towns were completely flooded. More than 10,000 homes were lost. Airport, railroad, barge, and road transportation was halted for weeks or even longer. Fresh water and sewage treatment plants were severely compromised. Des Moines was without fresh water for nearly two weeks.

CONVERGENCE

By the end of July, the Mississippi and Missouri rivers joined forces and moved south. More than 1,000 levees were destroyed or topped. At more than 600 points, rivers were flooded at the same time, flooding an area 450 miles long by 750 miles wide. That's more than 325,000 square miles of destruction. The Mississippi River alone flooded for about 200 days and rose 20 feet above flood level. By the time the waters fully receded in October, the human casualties were relatively low, but damaged property would take years and years to rebuild.

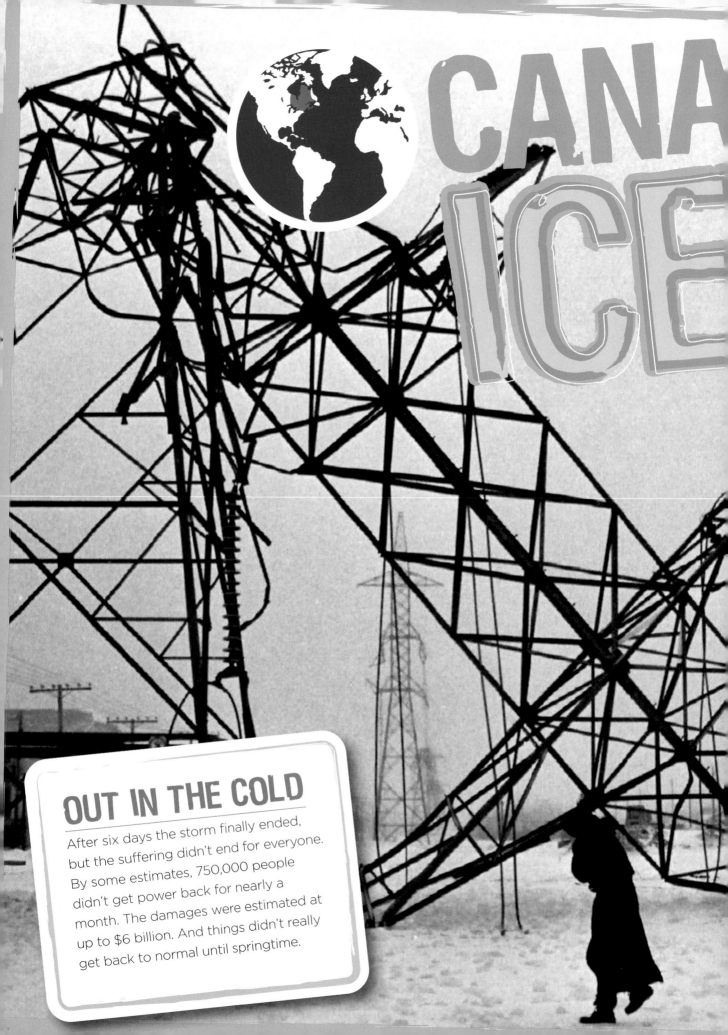

CANA
ICE

OUT IN THE COLD

After six days the storm finally ended, but the suffering didn't end for everyone. By some estimates, 750,000 people didn't get power back for nearly a month. The damages were estimated at up to $6 billion. And things didn't really get back to normal until springtime.

IAN 1998
STORM

Rainstorms bring crops. Snowstorms bring skiing. But ice storms bring only discomfort, fear, and danger. When a huge ice storm crippled Canada and the northeastern United States from January 4 to 10, 1998, it left tremendous damage in its path. Freezing rain is common up north and generally melts soon after it falls, but not before a few people slip and cars crash. This storm, however, dumped freezing rain (rather than snow) for 3½ days before the temperature dropped sharply. The thick sludge stuck to everything and then quickly froze, leaving a heavy ice coating up to 4 inches thick.

Canada's New Brunswick, Quebec, and Ontario provinces were left in a state of emergency. The capital city of Ottawa was shut down. So was Montreal. Similar conditions froze northern New York state and New England. The weight of the solid ice toppled countless power lines, plunging more than 4 million people into cold and darkness for days or weeks. Without power, water couldn't be pumped. Pipes froze and exploded. Near the turn of the millennium, people were turning to candles and fireplaces for light and heat.

The brilliant crystal coating on every exposed surface was spectacularly beautiful and dangerously deadly. Branches seemed dipped in glass, which is why millions of trees fell, toppled by the weight of the ice. Roads, bridges, and tunnels were closed by fallen trees and other items, blocking even emergency vehicles. Buildings collapsed. Massive ice chunks began dropping from above, adding to people's fear. And what's more, it was cold outside.

2002

SUP

DAMAGED GOODS

The storm bent trees nearly in half and threw car doors, jet skis, and other large debris several miles. An explosion rocked the island's oil facilities. A floating dry dock broke loose and was destroyed.

RTYPHOON
PONGSONA

The photographs from space showed a giant swirl of clouds with a solid white center where Guam should be. This small Pacific island, a territory of the United States in the Northern Mariana Islands, was hammered in 2002 by a mighty supertyphoon. It was a great tropical cyclone whose name, Pongsona, will never be forgotten.

On December 4, Pongsona was labeled a tropical storm located 1,000 miles southeast of Guam. It was typhoon season in the Pacific, so the 70 mph winds were strong but not out of the ordinary. When the skies began to darken in Guam on December 7, residents were expecting something big to come to their small island. Windows were shuttered. Roof tiles were nailed tight. Evacuation shelters in hospitals and schools were set up and would eventually house about 2,300 people when the deadly winds came.

Pongsona hit Guam and other islands on December 8. Deadly Category 4 and Category 5 winds of at least 150 mph were reported. Gusts were clocked at more than 180 mph . . . that is, until the U.S. weather service's wind speed anemometers were destroyed. The colossal 40-mile-wide eye of the storm hammered Guam's well-populated northern portion for more than four hours. More than 2 feet of rain added to the damage.

The winds died down at last and moved northwest over the Pacific until they dissipated on December 12. By then more than 1,000 houses had been torn and crushed, and another 7,000 were damaged by the howling whip of the typhoon's wind. No electricity, telephone, water, or sewer systems were in full service for several weeks.

REPEAT OFFENDER

Five years earlier, supertyphoon Paka had made Guam a federal disaster area. Pongsona upped the ante and did it again.

2004 INDIAN OCEAN TSUNA

To imagine the formation of a tsunami after an earthquake, think about dropping a bowling ball into a bathtub. The ocean water reacted to the giant quake by rising in massive swells in every direction. The waves from these tsunamis rose up to 100 feet high, traveling great distances (up to 5,000 miles from the epicenter) before crashing onto land.

On the morning of December 26, 2004, the second-greatest earthquake ever recorded shook the coast of Sumatra, Indonesia. This 9.2-magnitude quake, which lasted a record eight to 10 minutes, shook the entire planet and triggered a hideous series of tsunamis. It immediately became one of the world's worst disasters, in which close to 230,000 people in 15 countries lost their lives and coastal communities all around the Indian Ocean were destroyed.

From the land the warning signs of the tsunami were clear: The waves receded from the shore, and foamy bubbles appeared. Many people were able to reach higher or safer ground. The tsunamis struck the shores like violent tidal waves, with about a half hour passing between peaks. After the first waves struck, people ran down to the beach in many areas to see the results up close. They didn't expect the third wave (which was the strongest), and so it was human curiosity that cost tens of thousands of lives. More waves continued to hit for a number of hours.

The devastation caused by these tsunamis is difficult to convey. Flood damage reached inland several miles in some places. Entire villages were washed away. More than 1 million people lost their homes. The victims had to be gathered and buried. Disease, hunger, and a lack of clean water compounded the misery of the survivors. Fishing communities were devastated, losing their prime source of food and income.

But one small hope prevailed. The world pulled together, forgetting its differences for a while, sending every kind of aid to the suffering and demonstrating again what humans can do when they really want to.

2005 HURRICA KATRINA

T he United States has seen its share of hurricanes, tornadoes, cyclones, and serious windstorms. But no storm in recent history has had a more horrific, deadly impact than Hurricane Katrina. On August 25, 2005, in the midst of the Atlantic hurricane season, Katrina struck Florida as a Category 1 (80 mph) storm. Then, as it moved across the Gulf of Mexico, Katrina grew in force until it became a Category 5 storm (greater than 155 mph)—one of the strongest hurricanes ever recorded.

When Katrina hit the northern end of the Gulf on August 29, many major Southern cities suffered enormous damage, including Biloxi, Mississippi, and Mobile, Alabama. But no city suffered as much as New Orleans, Louisiana. The city's levees, or restraining seawalls, keep Lake Pontchartrain from flooding the greater New Orleans area (which is mostly below sea level). Once storm surges reached higher than 28 feet, the levees would fail and the city would flood.

Heavy rains and storm surges did cause Lake Pontchartrain to rise and flood for several miles, wiping out homes, bridges, and four crucial levees. Soon most of New Orleans was flooded in up to 20 feet of water. Evacuation routes were almost all blocked off. Local, state, and federal authorities were called in, as well as every possible emergency responder. But the situation remained dire.

The combined size of the federal disaster areas totaled about 90,000 square miles. Tens of thousands of victims relocated to Houston, Texas, and across the country, with no clue as to when they might go back home. It's no wonder Katrina's assault was America's costliest natural disaster, with damages estimated at more than $80 billion.

STRANDED

About 20 percent of the population hadn't fled before the storm and would find escape nearly impossible. Up to a million people lost power. Thousands waited for help in attics and on rooftops.

LAGUNA BEACH LAND

T he winters in Orange County are almost always dry and pleasant. But in 2005, Southern California had an especially wet winter—the second wettest on record—with more than 27 inches of rain, including 11 inches in February alone. That's good news for thirsty plants, but bad news for expensive ocean-view houses perched on eroding hillsides.

On June 1, 2005, real estate in the exclusive Bluebird Canyon neighborhood of Orange County's Laguna Beach became a little less valuable. An early-morning landslide announced its arrival with the sound of trees shifting, lampposts snapping, wood cracking, plumbing moaning, walls crumbling, and houses tumbling down the canyon. Residents awoke to terrible tremors and sounds, expecting yet another California earthquake. Soon it was apparent that far

more was going on. Families hurriedly collected their children, their pets, and their most valuable portable possessions and fled their neighborhood. Driveways and roads buckled as some houses literally crashed onto their neighbors' below. Miraculously, only four people suffered minor injuries.

The landslide affected at least 29 homes. Some were completely destroyed, and others were more or less intact but lay at odd angles. One thousand people—the residents of 350 area homes—were temporarily evacuated. Yet this wasn't the first landslide in Laguna Beach. Three hundred homes were damaged in a 1998 landslide, and another 14 took the plunge in 1978. Yet the average price of a home in the neighborhood is still more than $2 million.

GLOSSARY

AFTERSHOCK: a minor tremor following a large earthquake in the same region

ALTITUDE: the height of an object above land or sea level

ANEMOMETER: a device that measures and records the force or speed of the wind

ARID: an extremely dry climate

ATMOSPHERE: the layer of gases surrounding Earth

AVALANCHE: when snow, ice, rock or debris slide down a mountainside, often reaching speeds of 200 mph

BLIZZARD: a snowstorm with the following conditions: winds blowing at 35 mph or more and visibility less than one-quarter mile for three hours

COLD WAVE: a sudden drop in temperature within a 24-hour period

CYCLONE: strong winds moving about a low-pressure center

DAM: a barrier built across water to control the flow or raise the water level

DUST BOWL: a region that suffered from long droughts and dust storms

EARTHQUAKE: when Earth shakes due to underground movement along a fault line

EARTH'S CRUST: the outer part of Earth

ELEVATION: the height of something above land or sea level

EROSION: the process by which Earth's surface is worn away by wind or water

FREEZING RAIN: rain that falls as liquid and freezes upon impact to form a coating of ice on the ground or other exposed surfaces

FUJITA SCALE: measures tornado intensity (F0 to F5) based on the damage

GREAT PLAINS: natural grassland that stretches eastward of the Rocky Mountains from Canada to New Mexico and includes all or part of Montana, Wyoming, North Dakota, South Dakota, Nebraska, Colorado, Kansas, Oklahoma, Texas, and New Mexico

HEAT WAVE: a period of unusually hot weather lasting from several days to several weeks

HOT ASH FLOW: extremely hot volcanic ash and debris that roll quickly down the sides of a volcano

LANDSLIDE: when dirt and rock slide down a mountain or cliff

LAVA: molten rock that can be erupted from a volcano

LEVEE: an embankment that's designed to prevent a river from overflowing

MUD SLIDE: a landslide of mud

NATURAL DISASTER: any catastrophic force of nature not caused by human activity: avalanche, earthquake, flood, hurricane, lightning, tornado, tsunami, and volcanic eruption

PRECIPITATION: any form of water that falls to Earth's surface: drizzle, rain, hail, ice crystals, sleet, and snow

RICHTER SCALE: measures earthquake intensity on a scale of 1 to 10 based on seismic energy

SAFFIR-SIMPSON SCALE: measures hurricane intensity on a scale of 1 to 5 based on wind speed

SEDIMENT: solid inorganic or organic fragments that come from the weathering of rock and are carried and deposited by wind, water, or ice

SNOWPACK: the amount of annual accumulation of snow at higher elevations

SUPERTYPHOON: a typhoon with a wind speed of at least 150 mph

TIDAL WAVE: a huge destructive wave that sometimes follows an earthquake

TORNADO: a violent rotating column of air, often forming into a funnel cloud, reaching the ground

TSUNAMI: a fast-moving (up to 600 mph) ocean wave that travels over the open sea before hitting land